ON WHEELS

Also by Michael Holroyd

Non-Fiction
HUGH KINGSMILL
UNRECEIVED OPINIONS
LYTTON STRACHEY
AUGUSTUS JOHN
BERNARD SHAW
BASIL STREET BLUES
WORKS ON PAPER
MOSAIC
A STRANGE EVENTFUL HISTORY
A BOOK OF SECRETS

Fiction
A DOG'S LIFE

As Editor
THE BEST OF HUGH KINGSMILL
LYTTON STRACHEY BY HIMSELF
THE ART OF AUGUSTUS JOHN (WITH MALCOLM EASTON)
THE GENIUS OF SHAW
THE SHORTER STRACHEY (WITH PAUL LEVY)
WILLIAM GERHARDIE: GOD'S FIFTH COLUMN
(WITH ROBERT SKIDELSKY)

ON WHEELS
FIVE EASY PIECES
MICHAEL HOLROYD

Chatto & Windus
LONDON

Published by Chatto & Windus 2012

2 4 6 8 10 9 7 5 3 1

Text design by Matt Broughton. All illustrations by Finn Campbell-Notman.

First published in Great Britain in 2012 by
Chatto & Windus
Random House, 20 Vauxhall Bridge Road,
London SW1V 2SA

www.vintage-books.co.uk

Addresses for companies within The Random House Group Limited can be found at:
www.randomhouse.co.uk/offices.htm

The Random House Group Limited Reg. No. 954009

A CIP catalogue record for this book
is available from the British Library

ISBN 9780701187439

The Random House Group Limited supports The Forest Stewardship Council
(FSC®), the leading international forest certification organisation. Our books
carrying the FSC label are printed on FSC® certified paper. FSC is the only
forest certification scheme endorsed by the leading environmental organisations,
including Greenpeace. Our paper procurement policy can be found at
www.randomhouse.co.uk/environment

Printed and bound in Great Britain by Clays Ltd, St Ives plc

To Clara, Juliet and Courtney

His motor-car was poetry and tragedy, love and heroism. The office was his pirate ship, but the car his perilous excursion ashore.

Sinclair Lewis, *Babbitt*

CONTENTS

ACKNOWLEDGEMENTS

First of all I would like to thank my three dedicatees who have been my editors for over half-a-dozen years in Britain and the United States, piloting my last two books towards publication – and now this postscript. I also owe a great deal to my American agent Robert Lescher, whom I first knew as a publisher and who has with great generosity and care represented my interests for longer than either of us can accurately remember. I am also grateful to Elinor Cooper at A.P. Watt for her guidance and help. This volume has gained much from the gently comic pictures by the fine art illustrator Finn Campbell-Notman.

This is not my last book – I have already written that. It is a retrospective journey and an example, I believe, of nostalgic intertexuality.

ON WHEELS

INTRODUCTION

'Cars today are almost the exact equivalent of the great Gothic cathedrals,' Roland Barthes wrote in his *Mythologies*. Each was 'the supreme creation of an era', he argued, and both were appropriated by a whole population as magical objects. For my father and my grandfather – and also most of my biographical subjects – bicycles, motorbikes and cars were equivalent to our mobile phones and computers. They were significant parts of a magical new technology, full of excitement and mischief. I do not see the exploits and

1

misadventures-on-wheels of previous generations – let alone my own more tentative experiences – as banana-skin or custard-pie farce. If we laugh at our predecessors we laugh at ourselves: all of us have a place in the comedy. The fact that our fathers, having learnt to ride bicycles, were unable to pass on to their sons and daughters an immediate ability to ride them may be seen as an evolutionary defect. But it means that successive generations share very similar trials and errors. It is the machines that evolve and develop quickly – and we are continually left catching up with our inventions and discoveries.

Those who write about the past are often also referring to the present in the sense that they are focussing on human nature and the needs and anxieties that confront us. The past is frequently the same country as the present, or at least a similar country, and, with a little imagination, we can recognise ourselves in the world of our mothers and fathers, even our grandmothers and grandfathers. But the future, where all our hopes are fixed, is more difficult to recognise. My biographical subjects were all born in the nineteenth century. They opposed aspects of the Victorian ethic – sex, religion, politics – and hoped for a more tolerant, liberal culture in the century that was to produce two world wars.

Many of our inventions in the late nineteenth and early twentieth centuries gave us the ability to travel further and at greater speed. More recent technology enables us to communicate with people far away without travelling at all. I responded to the impetus of speed and can boast of having had penalty points put on my driving licence for travelling too fast (35 mph for example near Oxford). I also enjoy watching Formula One on television – I find that (like the athletic violence and painless deaths in some thrillers) the grunting, monotonous, hypnotic parade of cars circling round and round the track calms me. Do I understand the engaging complexities of soft, intermediate and hard tyres or the mystery of KERS (Kinetic Energy Recovery System) and DRS (Drag-Reduction System)? No I don't. But I like many things I don't understand such as the ever-expanding universe, the bewildering nature of time and the extraordinary way in which the latest, most powerful telescopes, magically combining ancient with modern vision, can search into the deep past. Such moments of glorious incomprehension give me pangs of what might almost be called religious elation.

But the recent revolution in technology arrived too late for me to grasp it satisfactorily. The media has become the message. I have a mobile but it was given to me without any written instructions and I am sadly at a loss in its company. I regard this mobile in much the same way as my grandfather approached his telephone. He knew that if it rang it would probably bring him bad news and if it didn't ring it was simply a waste of money. Occasionally, raising his voice to a shout, he was obliged to make a call himself, probably to the vet about one of the dogs. He did not enjoy these moments, finding it difficult to believe that anyone he could not see could actually hear him – yet at the same time suspecting that somehow everyone could overhear him after all and that his privacy was imperilled. He would have hated the notion that only nonentities who do not chatter enjoy private lives. As for my mobile, I reserve it for emergencies – and that means I have avoided using it to the point that I no longer know how to use it. At this stage it is little more than an inexpensive form of denial. So when at last the final great emergency arrives and the final question is asked, there will be no answer.

CHAPTER 1

SHORTLY BEFORE THE SECOND WORLD WAR

Shortly before the Second World War my aunt manoeuvred the family's black, eight-horsepower Ford into the garage of our new house at Maidenhead. I didn't see her do this (I was three or four at the time). But no one else could have done it – certainly not my grandfather or grandmother. My aunt seemed both conventional and eccentric, living a safe life in quiet anger, though able to take sudden initiatives which hinted at happier, more adventurous early years.

She loved and admired her father, but not her mother. The three of them had recently moved from a much larger house nearby and used the garage for storing everything that would not fit into their new home. The car rested in the middle of this chaos.

I came to live with my grandparents and my aunt a year or two after the start of the war and continued living there until I was twenty. The garage, with its mysterious and inviting conglomeration of objects, soon became a magic place for me. It was full of surprises, full of treasure. Crowded along the walls were all sorts of animals and birds in chipped Lalique glass: sparrows, fish, a fox, peacocks and dragonflies. My grandfather had been René Lalique's representative in Britain. In the late twenties and during the thirties he used to sell streamlined Lalique

figureheads – falcons, hawks, eagles, all sculpted in art-deco glass. Mounted on the front of expensive cars, these mascots were illuminated from within by small light bulbs. They were, the advertisements proclaimed, like 'the glittering ornaments in a lady's hat'. By the forties they nested, some of these birds, on the tops of cupboards and chests of drawers, in suitcases, behind ladders, and near the hooves of a half-demolished rocking horse. I made friends with these animals, taking them into the car where I would sit talking to them, keeping them warm.

Looking back, I am surprised that I never took hold of the wheel of the car and, with fierce engine noises, imagined myself winning tremendous races. In fact I thought I was sitting in a special armchair rather than at the wheel of a car. After all, it was never taken out of the garage and I never saw it move – it simply wasn't that sort of car.

The treasure I found huddled against the walls included pictures by Lewis Baumer and Anna Zinkeisen, illustrated books and catalogues, statuettes, paperweights and a bowler hat belonging to my aunt. I would carry some of these gems into the car and place them on the back seat where they would wait for me to come back. My grandparents soon got used to my being there and, once they knew I was safe, were pleased I had a room of my own. Otherwise I was a worry to them. When I was wandering around the house I would sometimes hear them cry out: 'What shall we do with the boy?' It was a question they never satisfactorily answered.

But I knew what I was doing. My

best discovery in the garage was a large radiogram on which I played some of my aunt's scratchy and discarded records. They were mostly tunes from the twenties and thirties: 'Miss Otis Regrets', 'Dinner for One Please, James', 'Who's Sorry Now?'. The dusty and uneven sound from these old records seemed to intensify a sense of poignancy that I came to understand only fifty years later when I wrote a family memoir and discovered the lost love that overshadowed my aunt's later life.

I would also play the wireless and began listening to classical music: Beethoven, Rossini, Schubert and Tchaikovsky. Sometimes I became so excited by what I heard that I had to climb out of the car and stride up and down the garage waving my arms high in the air as if surrendering to the music, as if conducting these symphonies and operas. In retrospect it seems to me that this car was my place of education, my seat of learning. I would go to the public library at the other end of town and bring back books by Conan Doyle, H.G. Wells and Rider Haggard, reading them by day in the car and by night more traditionally in bed with my torch.

I travelled between the library and the house on my bicycle – much to my grandmother's agitation. She would lean far out of her bedroom window, moaning softly, until she saw me turn the corner and come into view, when she would multiply her moans so that I could appreciate the volume of her anxiety. When she caught sight of me showing off as I careered down the road with my hands outstretched, she was convinced there would soon be a disastrous accident. But there was very little traffic in those days and there seemed more chance of her falling from her window than of me falling off my bike.

This bicycle was the most exciting of my possessions – more exciting even than my airgun or chemistry set. I would pedal down the hill, round the town and on towards the river. One evening I went all the way to Henley and thought I saw Stanley Spencer painting in the churchyard among the graves. It was as if this bicycle, which could carry me to such distant places, was attached to our house by an invisible elastic band. Wherever I went, however far, it always brought me back.

After the war was over, my life began to change – and so did that of my parents. My mother, who was Swedish, had earlier wanted to take me off to Stockholm where

I would be safer, but my father, who had made me a ward of court, argued that I would be perfectly safe with my aunt and grandparents in Maidenhead, which was of little interest to the German bombers. By the end of the war they were divorced. My father (who had been stationed in France while in the RAF) married a glamorous French publisher in Paris, and my mother, back in London, married a Hungarian businessman (at least that is what I thought he was). All this made the edges of my life very uneven, odd and bewildering. The only place that retained a central security for me was this house with its garage in Maidenhead. I passed most of my holidays from boarding schools there with occasional excursions by train to see various new step-parents.

When my father returned from France,

he began driving all over England and Wales looking for work. Sometimes I went with him in his Zodiac or Zephyr. These were cars in which he took much pride at a period when there was little else to be proud of. He liked talking to me about their gears and engines, their speeds-per-second – and I liked listening to him as we whizzed along. He was a poignant optimist and enjoyed being on the move, hurtling merrily towards his disappointing destinations.

He also liked travelling back in time as he steered into this bleak future, and would tell me stories of the happy, affluent days when he was growing up in the large house at Maidenhead. I picked up the exaggerated notion that this house had teemed with attics and cellars full of cheerful servants. In the early years of the twentieth

16

century the family owned a carriage and pair, but in 1908 (the year after my father was born), they bought a modern automobile: the four-cylinder Allday Autocar manufactured by Alldays & Onions, the Pneumatic Engineering Company which (like my grandfather) later went bankrupt. The ex-coachman drove it during the week and my grandfather took over the wheel at weekends. But this new technology disturbed him and he did not drive it for long. Apparently the car had no 'self-starter' and had to be brought to life by turning a handle at the front. This procedure often got the better of my grandfather. According to my father, there was also a petrol tap that had to be turned on to allow the petrol to flow from the tank to the carburettor – a fact my grandfather usually forgot. When they were children my father and his

brother enjoyed hiding behind the garage and watching him struggling to start the car. I asked him if his mother, my grandmother, ever drove the Allday. 'Certainly not,' my father said. 'Though she was one of the most accomplished back-seat drivers in the country.' Only fast women, it seemed, drove cars before the First World War.

But this changed after the war. Both my mother and my aunt drove cars. I believe my aunt saw her little Ford (the car that later came to rest in our garage) as a means of escape – rather as I used my bicycle. In the early thirties she had fallen deeply in love with a charming fantasist who invented an imaginary life for himself, using his racing car and his yacht to get away from the inauspicious facts of his life. He loved trains and boats and planes (having been in the Royal Flying Corps during the First

World War). And he loved the romance of travel, the speeding, racing, moving on from or rising up above people close to him whose existence he denied: such as the living parents he pretended had died in a car crash and the series of women he had married, left and forgotten. He kept his fast car and a little biplane at Brooklands, the famous motor-racing track in Surrey, and collected silver cups to show the many races he was supposed to have won. My aunt had to drive some sort of car if only to keep up with him, to keep him in sight. But he went abroad during the Second World War and married a young Italian girl in Rome – after which my aunt did not need the car or the records they had played. In a sense, they were her gifts to me.

At school my mother used to arrive in a

wonderful blue Buick that belonged to her
Hungarian husband. It had a dickey at the
back where I could sit in the open air with a
friend as my mother drove us off for lunch.
I was immensely proud of this car, but it
vanished after my mother's next divorce.
She liked cars but preferred to be driven by
other people.

My father, however, wasn't at all keen
on being driven by other people: he didn't
feel safe with them. This was probably
why, though he liked talking to me about
cars, he never suggested teaching me to
drive one. His divorces and remarriages in
the 1950s and 1960s didn't slow down his
driving. During the period when he lived
alone in Surrey, I went down by train at
weekends to see him and he would often
drive me over to Maidenhead to visit my
grandparents and my aunt. Sometimes,

when the weather was fine, he took them on excursions into the country – though my aunt, whose main occupation was walking her dogs, never joined us. I would go into the garage and see my old alma mater. Everything was as it had been, nothing had changed. I found these visits both comforting and disturbing.

In less favourable weather my father enjoyed driving me to meet several women in Surrey with whom (possibly unknown to them) he was contemplating marriage. They came and went over the years, these women, to my father's evident surprise – and also mine. Sometimes, to my embarrassment and theirs, I muddled up their names. All this seemed good material when in the late fifties I began writing a novel. It was frankly autobiographical and the character based on my father was often seen in his car. 'It was always a bit of a relief to be at the wheel and ponder over things in comparative peace ...' I wrote in my father's voice. I measured his drive to the office by the miles he covered, breaking up his thoughts into sections divided by his mileage: *Two miles ... Four miles ... Seven miles* etc until the twelve-and-a-half-mile journey was completed. The narrative of his journey back from the office in the evening was divided by the red, amber and green traffic lights that interrupted his journey. On this return journey he is racing another car. 'The two cars roared and jumped forward, slowed momentarily as the gears were crashed down, and then shot on again, wheel to wheel,' I wrote. It is true that my father resented being overtaken by other cars. In this fictional race between the two cars he slows down a long way before the red light and then accelerates as it is about to turn to amber, shooting ahead of his rival. 'Yes he had done it. She would never catch him now. He grinned to himself, a song rose in his throat and he began humming … A fine-looking female, though, he thought with a tinge of sadness.' He had won the race but in the excitement had not recognised the driver in the next car as his ex-wife, a character based on my mother, who is trying to signal to him – possibly about me.

I gave the typescript of this novel to my father to read and he was extremely angry. If I published it, he said, he would have to leave his job – no one who drove like this was safe on the roads, no one would employ him. He had not realised how much I disliked him – and the rest of my family. This was a most painful time for both of us.

I offered to rewrite the objectionable scenes. He said it was all objectionable, every page, and he wrote to my publishers promising to take them to court if they brought out the book. So it was never published in Britain – though it later appeared in America and I was able to use the money I made from it to help my father out of his gathering financial problems.

CHAPTER 2
DURING MY TWO YEARS IN THE ARMY

During my two years in the army as a National Serviceman I was appointed, rather incautiously, as the regiment's MTO (Motor Transport Officer). No one seemed to mind that I didn't have a driving licence – later on I was told I could have awarded myself one. But I suffered from what I now consider to be an enviable lack of self-esteem in such matters. It never occurred to me that one day I might actually drive or own a car. In fact I did not learn to drive until my mid-thirties. I was taught

26

by Philippa Pullar with whom I was living in the early 1970s. She had a house on the Kent coast at Deal and a flat in west London, travelling between the two places in her monster of a car. Once it must have been a proud and stately Austin but over the years it had evolved into a stubborn, bad-tempered beast with its own ideas of where it wanted to go. Philippa used it as a kitchen cupboard on wheels, filling it with fruit, flowers and vegetables, coffee and tea, loaves of bread and overflowing bowls of soup. There was also room for the cats, several guinea pigs in their cardboard boxes and even her two young sons. I can still hear their voices: 'Are we there yet? . . . Are we there yet?' Much of our time was anxiously spent in stationary queues of traffic on the M2 which was then in the process of being constructed. The car snorted, stalled, shook and blew out volumes of smoke, as if advertising our anxieties.

Philippa's driving experiences were very much at odds with my father's. I remember her telling him a story about a memorable Russian party. They drank so much vodka, she explained, that it was lucky her car was out of order that night. She caught the last bus home, she told him, and ended the night in bed with the bus conductor. Turning to my father sitting opposite her in his suit, she exclaimed with some indignation: 'Really, my dear, it's easier to get oneself serviced these days than one's car!' My father, who usually enjoyed talking about cars, was speechless. Profoundly bewildered by Philippa and all that went on around her, he could never quite get his balance in her company.

It was in her ill-used vehicle that I

eventually learnt to drive. Philippa would
take me to Richmond Park and then hand
the car over to me. Except for weekends,
the traffic there was light and moved
at a steady 20mph like a perpetual convoy
in mourning. It was obvious to me from
the very beginning that driving cars
was impossible. Human beings simply
weren't designed for it. For example,
how could they – how could I – manage
the three pedals (clutch, break and
accelerator) when I had only two feet?
It would take uncounted years for us to
evolve into coherent motoring creatures.
Technology had outstripped natural evolu-
tion. As for myself, it seemed unlikely
that I would be able to avoid the cars that
came flying so slowly towards us simply
because someone had painted a white line
in the middle of the road. Have you heard

of anything more ridiculous? Some of the oncoming traffic, of course, I could miss with great concentration and a slice of luck, but certainly not all of it, not every single one – that was asking too much.

Philippa's car responded very sensitively to my apprehensions, lurching ahead, and then shyly stopping whenever another car came into sight. These other cars seemed aware of our difficulties, sounding their horns, like excited elephants, in sympathy. After my first ten minutes at the wheel I was exhausted and had to lie down amid the carrots and cabbages on the back seat. But Philippa persisted. She wasn't going to drive to and from Deal all the time with me as a perpetual passenger. So I struggled on round Richmond Park sometimes creating havoc in the solemn mourning parade but gradually joining it, enjoying it.

Back home at night I studied the motoring literature and before long began to congratulate myself on becoming a scholar of the road, able to recite the number of yards it took to come to a halt at various legitimate speeds and to use a range of vigorous hand signals to attract the attention of other motorists. Nevertheless I felt nervous about my test.

The trouble was my driving instructor. I had taken some fifteen lessons from this man who reminded me of a peculiarly fierce sergeant major let loose from the army. Following him from his office to the car, I lost confidence as a pedestrian. His kerb-drill, shoes gleaming one inch from the pavement's edge, eyes swivelling right and left, was an awesome spectacle. When he turned sharply into other streets he made strange gestures with his

shoulders and elbows like the hand signals of someone without hands. Struggling along behind him, I began colliding with people. It was not a good beginning.

As pedestrians my instructor and I did not fraternise, did not even talk to each other, until we came sharply to a halt beside the car. Then he made an about-turn and addressed me: 'This', he said, 'is the car.' I nodded in agreement.

The first lesson was a very preliminary affair. Like dogs we circled the waiting vehicle, while my instructor pointed out features of interest to me: windows, doors, lights, bumpers and so on. Then we came to the soul of the lesson: entering, and exiting from, the car. I got in; I got out; and in again and out again. I did this on the nearside and the offside. I locked and unlocked the doors from inside and out. It was laborious work. As a mere passenger, I had never realised what a complex business this getting in and out of a car should be.

'DSM next,' my instructor said. This sounded dangerous to me. In fact DSM turned out to be Door, Seat and Mirror. I manipulated the windows endlessly up and down, and, like a dentist, adjusted the driving seat to its extremities, sitting at attention next to my instructor one minute, lying adjacent to him the next, and strapping myself in energetically at his command. During these exercises I was allowed short rest periods in which we discussed distilled water, tyre pressures and other vital matters. I mastered the milometer, speedometer, windscreen wipers, horn, oil gauge and (rather unnecessarily I thought) the brakes:

but we still had not moved. The dust was gathering on us. We seemed fated to be road furniture, never traffic. I could see no destination.

On my second lesson we did move the car: backwards at first (it was hardly progress) and then at last forwards. Milk floats, bicycles, old ladies and gentlemen from the previous century overtook us: but we were on our way.

I had booked my test before these lessons began and when the day arrived I knew what to do. All I had suffered during these long weeks of tuition, all the agony and boredom and dismay threaded over my fifteen lessons I concentrated into fifteen minutes and gave back. My examiner was a mild, moustached man. He did not know what he had done wrong. I came to his help. As I was able to demonstrate, he did almost everything wrong. He got into the car wrong, he sat wrong: he was an altogether unskilful passenger. At every move I put him scrupulously right, bundling him in and out and up and down. Nothing was too much trouble for me. Before we could start, I took it upon myself to prove that the car was worthy of the road. I checked and double-checked everything from the boot to the bumpers. When asked to drive forwards I did so – but only after violently adjusting the mirror, opening the window and giving a display of hand signals that any conjurer would have envied. There was so much to do I doubt we had time to move much more than a few hundred yards or so along the crowded London streets during the next half-hour. But it was an ageing experience. I had been well drilled in the theory of motoring and applied it rigorously. Under the weight of my performance, the examiner eventually cracked. His hands were trembling as he signed my certificate. By way of celebration I joined the AA (the Automobile Association not Alcoholics Anonymous).

I treated my test as if it were a miniature revenge comedy showing the pupil winning out against the teacher. In practice, I felt I was now better equipped to advance my career as a biographer. My first biographical subject, the novelist and biographer Hugh Kingsmill, did not drive a car – or if he did I was unaware of it. But my next biographies became increasingly filled with motoring exploits – something of which I was unaware until recently.

The first benefit of using a car in the writing and research of my books was being able to reach places more easily and, at least as important, being able to hurry away from them when I wanted. I was no longer tied to train times and train connections, no longer dependent on other people's goodwill to deliver me to stations and bus stops. In those uncomplicated days, before congestion zones and visitors' parking restrictions, this was a wonderful new freedom.

The initial encouragement that Philippa Pullar gave me to drive a car, I passed on to Margaret Drabble in the early eighties shortly before we married. She had taken a couple of tests early in her life and, somewhat undermined by her mother ('the finest driver never to get a licence'), had settled down to become a connoisseur of public transport and a healthy walker. But she bravely accepted my invitation to teach her. My technique was very informal and relaxed. I found an empty track bordered by bluebells not far from a house she was renting in Somerset and would drive her there. Then I got out of the car, walked round and sat in the passenger seat, lying back and appearing to go to sleep – which could be looked on as a mark of confidence. Occasionally I would stir and murmur some helpful words such as 'we'd better take off the brake' or 'those windscreen wipers are always getting in the way'. When Margaret reached the end of the track, I would turn the car round for her and then go back to sleep in the passenger seat. So we travelled backwards and forwards until one afternoon I did not need to turn the car round – she could do it herself. According to her, I had some unusual opinions about driving. 'The accelerator is a safety device,' she remembered me telling her. 'Get away from trouble as soon as you can.' I also advised her, she claimed, never to park over a grating or an open drain or she would certainly drop her keys down it when trying to unlock the door. This, I apparently added, was far more likely and a more terrible prospect than a head-on crash. She described my encouragement as 'relentless'.

Margaret took her test at Burnt Oak in London. 'When we pulled to a halt, the examiner told me I had passed,' she wrote. 'I told him I hadn't. He told me I had. I burst into tears ... [and] staggered back to the hut where Michael was waiting, and he knew from my face it had all gone wrong.' I do not know which of us was the more pleased by the result. Because she judged it to be 'one of the most surprising events of my life', Margaret credited me with having been a miracle maker. 'He is wasted on biography,' she told readers of the *Daily Mail*.

Margaret soon became a more fluent driver, I believe, than I am. But then, one dark winter night in the snow, there was a serious incident: in short, the car vanished. We reported its theft to the police – but not before I had walked up and down several roads nearby to make sure we had not parked it somewhere else. I had once reported my own car as being stolen and then, to my surprise, walking back from the phone box along a parallel road, found it parked exactly where I had left it. The explanation I had to give the police was humiliating. I didn't want to go through that again. But this was a genuine theft. Then that evening I had a brainwave. Margaret had plumbed a special telephone into her car and I suggested that we ring its number. She was game (though privately she thought this rather a silly idea), so after a glass of wine I did ring her phone number and a male voice answered me with a 'Hello'. 'Who's that?' I asked. 'I'm the thief of course,' the voice replied – and I heard laughter in the car. Unfortunately I had no answer ready and later wished I had prepared an elaborate trap pretending I was speaking to a criminal friend and informing him where he could pick up his share of some money I had stolen (a substantial sum it was). I imagined the thief driving to the pick-up place and falling into the hands of the waiting police while handing back our car. Unfortunately this was only a dream.

But I did phone the police to ask whether they could trace the whereabouts of the car from this call. They said they couldn't – which I later discovered was untrue. But the thieves immediately abandoned the car after my call and we got it back the next morning – minus the phone.

CHAPTER 3

MY FIRST CAR

My first car was a daffodil-coloured DAF – made by the Dutch company that specialised in manufacturing lorries, trucks and cabs. It was an automatic car (which worked by a simple belt or what was technically known as 'variomatic transmission'). This solved what, in my student days as a driver, I had reckoned to be an insoluble problem: the impossibility of dealing with three pedals with two feet.

Having no clutch pedal for changing the gears, my new DAF was fitted with only a brake and an accelerator: in my opinion the numerically correct arrangement. Reputed to be rather slow, the DAF was not a car that appealed to young sportsmanlike drivers, and was sometimes ridiculed as having been made for elderly men and women who couldn't drive. It suited me fine.

In 1975, having completed a biography of Augustus John, I drove my DAF across Wales and on to the Fishguard ferry that took me to Ireland. Here I began my research into the life of Bernard Shaw. I lived for over a year in the Rathmines district of Dublin, not far from Upper Synge Street where Shaw was born. I was also close to the larger house at Hatch Street where the Shaws later moved. Most days

I would drive to the National Library of Ireland that housed, among other Shavian material, the manuscripts of Shaw's early (much-underrated) novels. I also went to the National Gallery of Ireland which had a welcoming statue of GBS outside the front door and which contained many pictures (including works by Goya, Tintoretto, Fragonard and Joshua Reynolds) bought with the money Shaw had left to the gallery in his Will.

I particularly enjoyed driving to places in the country that had a special significance for Shaw during his early formative years. The most striking of these places was Dalkey Hill, some nine miles south of Dublin. When, at the age of seventy-five, Shaw was asked to name the happiest hour of his life, he replied: 'When my mother told me we were going to live on Dalkey Hill.' He belonged to an unconventional family: there were his two sisters, their mother, a rather obsolete father called George who was given to bouts of heavy drinking and, among all these Protestants, a musical 'genius' who was a Catholic and who was also called George. GBS sometimes questioned himself as to which George he had been named after. He felt, as it were, unsure (un-Shaw). In the 'awful little kennel' where he lived as a child in Dublin this Protestant-Catholic household, combined with the dubious reputation of the second man, George Vandeleur Lee, was highly embarrassing. But at Torca Cottage on Dalkey Hill where they all moved in 1866 when 'Sonny', as he was called, was aged ten, these embarrassments seemed to float away and vanish above the natural beauty of the place:

'its canopied skies such as I have never seen elsewhere in the world', he later wrote.

The front garden of their cottage overlooked Killiney Bay and the back garden Dublin Bay: and between the garden and those bays stretched a wonderland of goat-paths and gorse slopes down which Sonny would run to the sandy beaches below. Over a hundred years later I parked my DAF nearby, hiding it carefully behind some bushes so as not to encroach upon this vision of the past. Then I walked over the slopes where he had run and looked across towards the two great bays between Howth and Bray Head and down to the shore known as White Rock where Sonny plunged into the sea.

How much can travelling to places where their subjects lived help biographers? On his long walk through the Cevennes in pursuit of R.L. Stevenson and his donkey – a heroic wheel-less quest – Richard Holmes describes crossing a bridge at Langogne under the impression he was walking precisely in Stevenson's footsteps – and then looking across towards an old, broken bridge covered with ivy fifty yards downstream that he realised Stevenson had actually crossed in the late 1870s. Holmes accused himself of having been 'too literal-minded'. The biographical process, linking the past and present, is more subtle and imaginative than simple self-identification. It is a continuous dialogue of discovery between the writer and the subject, Holmes argues, between the living and the dead. As for myself I am not sure I could very easily point to sentences or paragraphs I would have written differently had I not been to special places such as Dalkey Hill or the Great Southern at Parknasilla, an extraordinary turreted hotel on the coast of Kerry where Shaw wrote *Saint Joan*. This was, I saw, a place of long sea views and intricate walks along the fingers of land that point into the Atlantic. I walked between the ferns and fuchsias, rock and rhododendron, to burnt-out castles that Shaw had seen while writing his play – the light, the air, the landscape: those things without which 'I cannot live', says Joan at the conclusion of her trial.

This sense of intimacy with a landscape or architecture might not add to the factual evidence of my research, but I believe it changes the tone and validity of what appears on the page. It may also bring a scene closer to the reader and introduce the equivalent of what Philip Larkin called the magical, rather than the meaningful, content. The same is true, I think, in the handling of manuscript letters and journals that put the biographer almost literally in touch with the men and woman who wrote those pages years before.

That evening, after walking up Dalkey Hill, I went to see the Irish playwright Denis Johnston who had known and corresponded with Shaw. His house looked out across one of the great bays facing towards Dalkey Hill and seemed to give the evening a special harmony. In any event, Denis Johnston suddenly decided to take me out to dinner. We went to his club. But unfortunately my casual outfit as a new motorist agitated the management of the club: in short, I was not wearing a tie. Nor was there a spare tie on the premises. We stood around politely wrestling with the problem. Eventually it was solved by allowing us to dine behind a screen that concealed the inadequacy of my dress. Years later I saw Denis Johnston's daughter, the novelist Jennifer Johnston, who told me this tête-à-tête dinner had become a favourite family story – almost a legend.

Dublin was not kind to my car. When England played Ireland at rugger, or any other sport, the enthusiastic Irish crowds liked to celebrate their victory by dancing on my DAF; and if Ireland lost, they vented their anger on it. Whatever the result, when I looked out of the window next morning, I saw, instead of my modest daffodil-coloured vehicle, something that resembled an experimental, low-strung, sports car. The offence of course, was my English number plates. I appealed to the Irish

seminary at the end of the road to let me park my car in its spacious grounds on international sports days, but they refused me this protection. I remember feeling shocked by what seemed to me such an unchristian turning-away – perhaps they would have been more generous had my car been grander. But I put aside these ill thoughts and, after taking a new driving test, I applied for an Irish number plate. Now all was well. When in Ireland, do as the Irish do.

Then I drove back through Wales to England – and again all was not well. I was stopped by the police and asked to open the boot of my car. They examined my luggage, looked through my books, my papers, my unlaundered clothes, then waved me on. And this happened every two or three weeks. I knew what it was to be an IRA suspect in London. So once more I went off to change my number plates – and somewhat to my surprise came back with a new car. With the money from my *Augustus John* and the contract for *Bernard Shaw*, I could afford a new car. I traded in my DAF and drove back in a blue automatic Honda Accord that I saw in the salesroom. And out of habit, I have continued to use Hondas for the rest of my driving life. I am hoping one day to be paid handsomely by the Honda company for my loyalty.

By now my mother, having left her third husband, had gone to live in South America with a wealthy admirer who manufactured motorbikes. She wrote to me reassuringly to say that if and when all else failed (she was referring to my books), I could join her in South America and help manufacture motorbikes myself. This was an opportunity I missed and it was my mother's relationship with the millionaire that eventually failed. Back in London, she became severely ill and had a breast removed in hospital. Though she was too unwell to travel anywhere, let alone drive a car, she asked me to fill in a form that permitted her to travel by car without using a safety belt. She felt this licence, like a badge, gave her status. But the days of safety were sadly over.

I did not tell my father much about my car. He knew I had one and occasionally asked me about it. But I sensed that he wanted to hold on to the authority of being the only member of the family who drove. When I told him mine was an automatic, he was relieved. Automatic cars were not real cars in his vocabulary.

'I like to change my own gears,' he said, 'rather than have them changed for me in Detroit or Tokyo.'

By this time he had only intermittent jobs and drove his Zodiac round the country much less frequently. He had also pretty well given up driving me through Surrey to meet the clutch of women he thought might marry him. After his last divorce had been made absolute, he settled down with a miniature German police dog for company. It went for walks with him and it went for drives, often sitting on his lap with its paws on the wheel. I'm not sure whether this was responsible for some of his accidents. I remember visiting him in the cottage hospital near his home in Ewell when his leg was fractured after he had crashed into a bollard. He told me, with some pride, that he had been first off from the lights and if some bloody fool hadn't recently moved the bollard for no good reason he would have left the other car far behind.

During the war my aunt had driven a library van round the Home Counties delivering books to German and Italian prisoners, captivating them (as I imagined when a child) behind the barbed wire with her choice of thrillers and adventure stories. I remember her co-driver, Miss Terry of the chocolate family, telling me that it was safer driving at night because you could see the lights of oncoming cars before they appeared round the corners. When the war was over my aunt gave up driving and disappeared with her dogs on long walks across the fields, past the church, over the hills, and far away. The dogs would come back exhausted. My aunt needed these walks, needed a sense of liberation. After her dogs died she still strode out, a solitary figure in the landscape who appeared to be exercising a ghost-like pack of invisible and unruly animals. Then one day, about a mile from home, she had a stroke and was carried back to the house on a milk float. After she left hospital, we sold the house at Maidenhead and moved her into a ground-floor apartment in the building my father occupied at Ewell. She was to be paralysed for the rest of her life but moved about quite neatly and ingeniously in a wheelchair. My father, who was becoming forgetful, thought her rather lazy.

I remember driving my Honda Accord behind my father's Ford Zodiac on our last journey from Berkshire into Surrey, from Maidenhead to Ewell. I saw him wandering crazily all over the road with his dog apparently at the wheel. Then it was I

realised that in future I would have to drive him where he wished to go. For safety I insisted that he and the dog sit on the back seat of my car while I chauffeured them around. At first it was difficult for him to accept this change of status. He was not an easy passenger, his feet and arms moving as if he were in control of my Honda, in control of me. But one day, as the dog bounced frantically between us making it difficult to communicate, he suddenly shouted: 'They're not so bad after all, these automatic cars.' He looked a bit embarrassed and struggled to get out of the car, though we were still in mid-journey. But I knew this was his way of thanking me for what little I could do for him in old age.

CHAPTER 4
IN THE SIXTIES

In the sixties I wrote and published my
Life of Lytton Strachey. Strachey didn't
drive a car but he knew very well the
romance and potency of them, their effect
on people's imaginations. In 1922, at a
particular crisis in the complex emotional
climate in which he lived, he made the
gift of a car to the burly Ralph Partridge
(who was in love with Dora Carrington,
a lesbian who had fallen passionately in
love with the homosexual Lytton who

was greatly attracted to the heterosexual Ralph). This generous and imaginative gift brought a sudden stability and happiness to the intense drama of their lives. Ralph fortunately discovered he was 'a born motorist' and Carrington thought the new car 'a great joy. We go for lovely rides in it.' She was even more pleased when Lytton gave her a horse named Belle. 'I have never seen the landscape so lovely,' she wrote after her first fifteen-mile ride across Berkshire.

Between the two world wars it was usually the man who sat in the driving seat – a phrase that describes almost the entire social fabric of Britain. Women were not encouraged to drive, but they were expected to absorb some knowledge of motoring from their men-fellows. Occasionally these spots of information were socially useful. For example when Virginia Woolf met Violet Trefusis's mother, Alice Keppel, the mistress of Edward VII, in the early thirties, the two of them had some difficulty in sustaining a polite drawing-room conversation and were falling into a pit of silence when motor cars suddenly rose to their rescue. They had no interest in cars, but they could repeat what they had heard others say – which was a safe passage through social embarrassment. Mrs Keppel strongly recommended 'six cylinders though I know some people think four are less trouble'. And Virginia Woolf was able to respond by enthusiastically pressing on her 'the *new Lanchester with the fluid fly-wheel*!'

There are, of course, some bold and unconventional women in my books. Vita Sackville-West seemed to use her car as an additional bedroom. Driving her friend 'Christopher' (born Christabel) over Westminster Bridge, she took her hand off the wheel and, touching her, declared that she was one of those rare people Vita really loved. At the end of their journey, she parked the car in a dusky side street in Tonbridge and gave her a lover's kiss. 'In all my dreams I had never dreamed of that,' Christopher wrote. But alas there were to be no more motoring adventures for her.

Some of the men in my books, such as the actor Henry Irving, died too early to join the motor revolution. His partner on stage, Ellen Terry, who lived into the late 1920s, preferred a horse and cart to a car. But in the following decade Ellen's daughter Edy Craig owned a much-loved car called Belinda, which she would fill with her women friends. Before long, however, she wisely handed over Belinda's wheel to a niece who careered round Kent with great gusto, like a motorist, it was said, 'of Brooklands calibre'.

Remembering my grandfather's inabilities as a driver, I was not surprised to learn while writing my family memoirs that his mistress (who almost bankrupted our family) left him in the 1930s to marry a man who, despite his infantile paralysis, had a dangerous passion for fast cars and owned five luxury Packards. 'One foot on the accelerator, one foot in the grave,' he was fond of saying. It must have been a relief when this semi-paralysed car maniac got a steady job as consultant for the Rolls-Royce coachwork.

But the most exciting motorist among the significant minor characters in my

books is undoubtedly Catherine Till, who steered me through part of my last book, *A Book of Secrets*, while at the same time doing her own research. No one, I prophesy, will ever outpace her. She took me all round Yorkshire while I was working on my book, but it was not until we went to Italy together that she showed me the full range of her motoring abilities. Our first test was getting out of Naples airport. The car we had rented was parked so close to other vehicles that I could see little chance of entering it – except perhaps through the windows. I don't know how she did it, but with the skill of a contortionist Catherine managed to force her way in. She then set about experimenting with the Italian gears until the car, like a frightened animal, jumped backwards, almost knocking me to the ground.

Not knowing which direction to take I suggested we stop to read the road signs. This struck Catherine as an awfully tame suggestion. I had a map, a small map, but unfortunately it covered the whole of Italy and our fifty-mile journey to Ravello (it turned out to be somewhat longer) was hardly visible. Reading the signs, which Catherine politely allowed me to do, was a more complicated business than I had expected since most of them pointed to restaurants. When we did eventually reach Ravello, I wrote up an account of our journey in case the vividness of the experience should fade (in fact it has never faded).

'Catherine decided to take the Salerno road south which, I point out rather unhelpfully, is also the road north to Rome. At this unpalatable news the gears of the car begins to complain loudly, jerking us suddenly forwards and then backwards. "Am I in second or third?" Catherine demands, and I bend down, still holding my map, trying to find out. Doing a U-turn on the flat roof of an apartment block, I hear her whispering quietly to herself like a prayer: "*Piano. Piano.*" But I couldn't hear anything. Somehow, in spite of all obstacles, we reach the autostrada, fling indiscriminate coins at the guard, then rev up and sail on. "Where are we now?" Catherine asks and then, taking both hands off the wheel and pointing at the sky, she cries out: "There's Vesuvius!" That's fine but where is Ravello? My hands move frantically across the map. I call out names and Catherine politely corrects my pronunciation. It has become a language lesson at high speed. At last we see a sign to Ravello and lose ourselves in a maze of indistinguishable streets. We stop and ask directions from a girl with a dog: neither of them admits to knowing anything. We climb into the mountains veering one way then another, sometimes on two wheels. Catherine encourages the poor car as if it were Basil, her horse. She is enjoying herself. At one hazardous moment high up she asks me whether I would prefer to be crushed against the rock face or fall to my death in the valley. I choose the rock face. "Do keep reminding me", she reminds me, "that they drive on the right in Italy." Much of the time we compromise and drive in the middle. But Catherine is more confident in the mountains. When I say "We turn right here" she answers that it doesn't matter – and she is right. Suddenly all roads lead to Ravello. We are there.'

*

71

The first serious and determined motorist among my biographical subjects was Augustus John. In his early years at the turn of the century he had taken enthusiastically to bicycles. As he rushed along the roads on his bike, he presented a spectacular figure: so spectacular that, to be on the safe side, men and women briefly catching sight of him would sometimes cross themselves. At one village in France where he stopped, the local priest had invited him to take the principal role in their Passion Play. But he modestly refused after hearing that, in the heat of the occasion the previous year, Christ had been stabbed and landed up in hospital.

But it was with motor cars that John was to reveal the full flavour of his character. 'It can't be denied that there is something gorgeous in motoring by night at 100 kilometres an hour,' he wrote in 1911 after escaping across Europe from August Strindberg's second wife, Frida. A couple of years later, when painting in the west of Ireland, he tried out Oliver St John Gogarty's canary-coloured Rolls-Royce and decided that he must have a car himself. But it was not until 1920 that, in exchange for a painting, he acquired a powerful two-seater Buick with yellow wheels and a dickey. After enduring a tedious half-hour lesson in London, he crowded it with friends and set off for Alderney Manor, his home in Dorset. Apart from barging into a barrel organ and apparently derailing a train, they had a successful journey down – despite the fact that, because John's lesson had never touched on the philosophy of gear changing, the car had been in first gear from start to finish.

All his family insisted on being taught immediately – in fact they taught each other and by nightfall the house was full of brand-new drivers. 'After that we always seemed to be whizzing,' one of John's sons remembered. 'In those days the roads were still fairly empty and motoring was a sport. We nearly always came up with another fast car, also on its way to town, and then we would race it for a hundred miles. No matter who was driving, we made it a point of honour not to be outdone, and we very seldom were. When our car and its rival had passed and repassed each other several times, emotion would work up to a white-heat, and every minor victory was the signal for wild hilariousness.'

These were great days for car enthusiasts. The John family's style of motoring was seen in its purest form whenever

Augustus himself took the wheel. In fine country on a good day, he was apt to forget he was driving at all, allowing the car to pelt on ahead while he stared back over his shoulder to admire the receding view. Indeed the car often performed better like this than when he bent upon it his absolute attention. Then, roaring like a maddened bull, it would sometimes mount hedges, charge with intrepid bursts of speed towards corners, or simply explode. Once, when hurtling towards a fork in the road, he demanded which direction to take, and, his passenger hesitating a moment, they bisected the angle, accelerating straight into a ploughed field until brought to a halt by the waves of earth. Another time he awoke to find himself driving through the iron gate of a graveyard.

The car soon began to present a

dilapidated appearance, like an old animal in a circus: the brakes almost ceased to operate, and the central mechanism could only be worked by two people simultaneously, the second taking off the handbrake at the precise moment when the first, manipulating the knobs, pedals and levers as if performing on an organ, caused the engine to engage with the wheels. But though he occasionally admitted the car to be suffering from a form of indigestion known as 'pre-ignition' or to be unaccountably off colour ('pinking somewhat'), John always loyally insisted that his Buick was 'still running very sweet'. It was true that sometimes, 'like a woman', the car refused to respond and had to be warmed up, cajoled, petted, pushed. Then she would jerk into life and, with her flushed occupants, drag herself away from this scene of humiliation to the cheers of voyeurs. In her most petulant moods she reacted only to the full-frontal approach. But once, when Augustus was winding up the crank (the car having been left in gear on the downward slope of a hill), she ran him down. His companion, a music critic, frantically pulling and pushing everything his hands and feet could reach, was carried out of sight.

Though accidents were plentiful, the Johns themselves seemed miraculously indestructible. They were, however, extremely critical, even contemptuous, of one another's skills. John's long-term common-law wife Dorelia refused to applaud his inspired cornering; while he irritably censored her triumphant use of the horn.

Towards motorists outside the family, though quietly dismissive of their abilities, they were nervously polite. Such courtesy was often useful in court. The biographer Montgomery Hyde, who happened to be passing one day, observed how John, coming out of his drive 'fairly rapidly', cannoned into a steamroller which was doing innocent repairs to the road outside his gate. John very correctly reported the incident to the police, who replied with a summons. In due course he appeared before the local Bench and was acquitted because, the magistrate explained, his manners were so vigorous and impressive.

As it whirled through the twenties and thirties, the car took on many aspects of John's character. It became in effect a magnified version of himself. He had done his most brilliant work, both as a draughts-man and a painter, during the fifteen or sixteen years before the First World War after which, despite a few memorable portraits – paintings of Thomas Hardy and Dylan Thomas, drawings of James Joyce and Delius – his lyrical talent faded. But his fame grew and, with his adventurous exploits in the car, he seemed to represent the 'have fun while we may' culture between the wars, gathering a darker and more sombre aspect when the Second World War began. In spite of all vicissitudes, his Buick continued somehow to function, though with increasing noise and pathos, until it was finally abandoned, upside down and panting horribly, somewhere near the West End of London.

CHAPTER 5

OUR UNIVERSAL FUTURE

Bernard Shaw believed that the most exciting evolutionary event during his lifetime had been the discovery of the road wheel – that at any rate was the conclusion I reached after fifteen years studying his work. His first experience of this wonderful circular object came at the age of thirty-nine when he began riding bicycles. 'I will do twenty yards and a destructive fall against any professional in England,' he wrote in 1895. 'I will not be beaten by that hellish machine.' Lying exhausted in a deep ditch one night, the moonlight filtering on to him through the revolving spokes of the wheels, he bravely concluded that bicycling was 'a capital thing for a literary man'.

For a dozen years the bicycle was a prime article of Shavian equipment. By increasing the efficiency of life (that is, increasing the pedestrian's few miles to almost a hundred miles in a day) the bicycle, which was attacked as a terror to horses and a temptation for women, became a symbol of modernity. As such it was wheeled by way of metaphor and analogy into many Shavian arguments.

In 1896 he was enrolled as the 621st member of the Cyclists' Touring Club and began pouring out information and advice about varieties of crack machines. His experiments were extraordinary. He would raise his feet to the handlebars and simply toboggan down steep places. Many of his falls, from which with black eyes, violet lips and a red face, he would prance away crying 'I am not hurt!', acted as trials for his optimism. After one appalling crash, he claimed that anyone but a vegetarian would have been killed; and nobody but a teetotaller could have mounted a bicycle again for six months.

'I shall take to motoring presently,' he wrote in the summer of 1908. He had already subjected himself to lessons by a professor of driving at the National Motor Academy and by the end of the year bought his first automobile, a 28–30 horsepower Lorraine-Dietrich with a detachable hind part. 'The lines of the car are uncommon,' reported *The Autocar*. They became

a little more uncommon when Shaw's wife Charlotte bumped it gently into an obstruction (believed to be a gate), scattering the splashboards, paddle-box and other impedimenta.

Charlotte's career as a motorist was brief and as Shaw was rather too fond of reading in the car, they employed a chauffeur called Albert Kilsby. In Kilsby's opinion the De Dietrich was 'a proper bugger' to start. Shaw found it awkward to stop. The 'loud' pedal (otherwise known as the accelerator) was on the left with the foot brake on the right. In later years he faithfully kept the habit of treading on the right pedal to arrest his vehicles.

The two men, Shaw and his chauffeur, shared the driving fairly evenly. The De Dietrich was a car for all seasons and subjects: a philosophical vehicle that posed many questions. Shaw reported on its capacity to penetrate Swiss avalanches and its place in the future of Ireland; on its moral claims versus those of the road dog, and its tax-generating properties. Of its detachable wheels, movable hood and electric klaxon horn, its cork and brass, the invisible locks and variable speed dynamo, he grew pedantically fond. He still used the train for long political journeys, but for serious holidaymaking the car became essential.

Packing a copy of the Koran, the Shaws took it first to Tunisia and Algeria, Kilsby veering dramatically away from wonderful seas with islands rising out of their mirror-like waters and other magnificent mirages in which he could not bring himself to disbelieve. They tried out the Irish roads with an expedition to Lady

Gregory at Coole and an expedition to the Giant's Causeway. In 1910 the car took them for a spin through France, Shaw coming to the conclusion in a report for the Royal Automobile Club that, owing to the cambered roads it was impossible to pass anything without first coming to a halt. Motoring in France, he decided, was like driving along the roof of St Pancras Station. 'GBS does not allow us one moment of peace,' Charlotte complained. 'We are *harried* from place to place.' His diary lists some forty towns in France, Italy, Switzerland, Austria and Germany they passed through in their travels two years later.

The war came to their rescue, confining them to a series of theatre tours and purposeful Fabian Summer Schools in Britain. During the war, Shaw became

a fiery motorcyclist, gingering up his two-stroke machine that would hurtle away, bucking him off sometimes and landing on top of him. He took hypothetical instruction from the village chemist at Ayot St Lawrence on how to steer round corners, but could not bring himself to accept the theory that it was necessary to lean over at an angle while doing this. The chemist was impressed by his 'outstanding deficiency in mechanical sense'. The hints given to him on the art of reversing were of little use, Shaw taking half an hour to turn a corner backwards and demolishing some flowerbeds in the process. But the village grew proud of his road exploits. Local dogs, knowing him well, would play dead under his car while he anxiously crawled after them – when they would bounce out, barking triumphantly. Though reckless, he was always considerate, leaping out on to the road after a bump or crash and offering to pay all expenses and drive people home or to the hospital. He was especially chivalrous to the injured when the fault was theirs.

Later on, in the early 1930s, he was to introduce into the second act of his political extravaganza *Too True to be Good* a 'powerful and very imperfectly silenced motor bicycle' which emits 'a shattering series of explosions' as it careers over the sand dunes. It belongs to an insignificant-looking private soldier with an enormous name: Napoleon Alexander Trotsky Meek. He is Shaw's fantastical version of a military genius and his dramatic portrait of Lawrence of Arabia. He had given Lawrence a Brough Superior motorcycle named 'Boanerges' after the aggressively

self-assertive left-wing politician who
fancies himself as a strong man in Shaw's
previous play, *The Apple Cart*. But in 1935,
when racing home from Bovington Camp,
Lawrence swerved to avoid some boys on
bicycles, went into a skid and was thrown
over the handlebars to his sudden death at
the age of forty-six. Shaw took a desperately
optimistic view of this fatal accident. 'He
always dreaded pain and the idea of death
... and now, you see, he had got off without
knowing anything about it.'

At the end of the war Charlotte had engaged
Fred Day as their new chauffeur. He stayed
with the Shaws for thirty-one eventful
years. It was, he insisted, an interesting job.
He got to drive all manner of machines:
a Vauxhall, a Bianca with mechanical windscreen wipers, a straight-eight

Lanchester with a harmonic balancer which Shaw pretended was a musical contraption, a chocolate-coloured Rolls-Royce and finally a 25–30 horsepower Silver Wraith. You couldn't ask for more.

Shaw liked to ride in the front next to Day, sitting bolt upright with a cushion at his head. He would usually take the wheel until lunch. Charlotte always sat at the back where Shaw had designed a special upholstered seat for her in a compartment sealed from draughts and fitted with a heater. In this manner they toured the country, travelling very slowly when Charlotte was with them and very fast when she wasn't. Sometimes when visiting their friends they went by train, arranging for Day to make his way by road with their bags. It seemed to him a funny sort of logic, using a Rolls-Royce for carrying baggage.

Day was fond of his work and would 'do anything for Mr Shaw'. One afternoon Shaw noticed him give a small wave to a woman and child at a bus stop. 'Who's that?' Shaw asked. 'My wife,' Day answered. 'Stop!' Shaw commanded. 'Turn round. We must take them home.' Day had schooled his family never to recognise him when he was on duty. In those days it was 'not usual for the gentry to have anything to do with the staff. But Mr Shaw was different. He put his arm round her shoulders and helped her into the car. She was terrified.' Later on Shaw offered to pay for their daughter's training as a schoolteacher.

They postponed their most serious accident until Shaw and his wife went to South Africa in 1932. He was driving along the Garden route to Durban, negotiating 'several mountain tracks and gorges in a masterly manner', he remembered. Reaching a stretch of smooth straight road he 'let the car rip'. (When writing my Life of Shaw I drove along the same route and also let the car rip, glad that the road had been much improved in the fifty-year interval.) Shaw's car hit a bump and veered violently to the right. He twisted the wheel to the left, then transferred his foot to the brake – but it was not the brake, it was the accelerator. The old De Dietrich had come back to haunt him. By the time they came to a halt down a steep hill, Shaw had 'a clout on the jaw and a clip on the knee'. But Charlotte was badly injured and taken to hospital at Knysna. It took over a month for her to recuperate during which time Shaw wrote *The Adventures of the Black Girl in Her Search for God*.

After his eightieth birthday he pretty

well gave up driving. This was a relief for Fred Day. Increasingly he had been obliged to pull the wheel from Mr Shaw's hands crying 'Brake, sir!' or 'That will do, sir.' It was an anxious time. 'I was fully occupied trying to keep him out of trouble,' Day admitted. Shaw agreed. 'I don't know why on earth they let me have a driving licence at my age,' he complained one day after plunging into some oddly placed hot-water pipes in the garage.

In the concordance of Shaw's plays and prefaces there are some thirty entries for bicycles, over a hundred entries for cars and another fifty for motors of one sort or another. The most celebrated car in his plays appears in *Man and Super-man*. It is expertly driven through this 'Comedy and Philosophy' by a Cockney chauffeur named Henry Straker. He is a scientific socialist, the product of a Board School and polytechnic, cool, vigilant, proud of being a skilled engineer, never deferential to socially superior classes. He is the New Man at the beginning of the twentieth century, the man of technology who has arrived unnoticed while everyone was preoccupied with the New Woman – the woman of initiative who was replacing the Victorian Woman on a pedestal. Such characters embody modernity and made Shaw the idol of young playgoers who entered the Royal Court Theatre as nineteenth-century aesthetes and came out as twentieth-century radicals.

Shaw's life spanned an extraordinary historical period from the Crimean War to the Korean War. He was born before the publication of Darwin's *On the Origin of Species* and lived to see the dropping of the atom bombs on Hiroshima and Nagasaki. Believing that a writer's business was to mind everybody else's business, he involved himself in everything. He had a moral commitment to optimism that concealed a darker pessimistic instinct. What his addiction to cars and his creation of Straker represent is his belief in what was new and the miraculous possibilities awaiting later generations. If he were alive today you wouldn't get him off television, off Twitter, off Facebook. He would be equipped with the latest pads and pods, adapting email to his phonetic alphabet and prophesying our universal future.

ENVOI

Recently I sat on the top floor of a bus, right at the front – and was horrified. Something serious has happened since I was a child. I remember the excitement then of looking into a series of first-floor windows of houses as they sped by, and the sensation of hurtling forwards, then suddenly stopping, of miraculously missing other buses as they charged towards us with rows of children waving and silently shouting before we left them behind us. I would clamber up the stairs, holding on for life, and jostling with other children as I fought to gain a prized front seat. And when I succeeded it was as good as riding the dodgem cars when the fair came to town.

But it's all different now. Twice, when the bus abruptly turned corners as if throwing off a deadly pursuer, I was hurled to the floor and then surrounded by anxious men and women, mostly pensioners I believe, helping me up. It was humiliating – I actually thought that I heard some laughter from passengers at the back. Was it the driver's fault? Or perhaps it was the winter weather which had created so many potholes in the road along which we violently bumped and jolted. We also had to negotiate a series of roadworks that made the journey into an obstacle course – several times we mounted the pavement as we swerved round these barriers. One way and another it was all extremely uncomfortable. I blamed the hellish traffic, the appalling weather, the decline of the country into Third World chaos.

Or is it simply that I am less young than I was?

I still drive a Honda, but now I have a permanent companion – a navigation device that speaks to me in a woman's voice, telling me where to go and what I should have done. Sometimes I cannot help replying to her. But of course she takes no notice and once I have switched her on I cannot find any way of switching her off. It's not that I take offence at being told what to do by her. No, certainly not. It's positively good to be advised, as I rev up the engine and drive off, that I have forgotten to take off the handbrake or left the boot open.

Sometimes I pretend that I am testing her
– and throw her a quiet compliment on
having spotted my deliberate mistake. But
at other times she is simply wrong. I do
not hesitate to use that word. Wrong. For
example she believes that I live on the other
side of the road. I cannot cure her of this.
I know the way back home – at least from
some places nearby I do – and she tells me
to go right when I always go left. Once, out
of politeness and to humour her, I did go
right and I found a perfectly good new way
home. But it's no better than my way and
I prefer my way – it is more friendly than
hers. Nor do I want her getting the better
of me all the time. I have gone her way and
she has never guided me home by my way
however many times, at my calm insistence
and disobeying her obstinate instructions, I
have taken the trouble to take her home my

way so that she could understand it. She is extraordinarily insensitive and simply will not listen, look and learn. Not that I have lost my temper. Not once. Not really lost it. But she suffers from a disease called unsympathetic fallacy syndrome. It is an acute case – and I have told her so.

In any event I am driving less than I used to do. It's not simply the arguments I've had with my navigator. Underneath our difficulties we are friends, good friends, for much of the time. But I have come to like trains because I can do two things at the same time in them: eat a sandwich, read a book and look at the country with its horses, sheep and cows as they flow past. Actually that's three things. On the other hand I can make quite a mess of a sandwich when I am driving and often have to brush up and wash down my clothes afterwards.

Last year I drove just 3,000 miles, where once I managed almost 10,000. This year I reckon it will be even less. And I am too old, and frankly too dangerous, to go wobbling around on bicycles, especially bicycles supplied by bankers. As for roller skates, which I loved as a child, I doubt if they will feature in my second childhood. It will be back to the pram, or something like it. I shall stretch forth my hands, and another shall gird me: and I will be carried where I do not know.

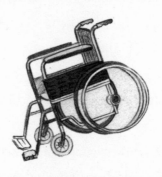